Cosmic Musings

Contemplating Life beyond Self

Larry Bell

Larry Bell

Cosmic Musings

Other books by Larry Bell:

Scared Witless: Prophets and Profits of Climate Doom
*Climate of Corruption: Politics and Power behind the Global Warming
Hoax*

STAIRWAY PRESS—SEATTLE

Cover Design by Chris Benson
www.BensonCreative.com

STAIRWAY⫢PRESS

www.StairwayPress.com
1500A East College Way #554
Mount Vernon, WA 98273 USA

I wish to thank the wonderful staff at Houston's Methodist Hospital who recently intervened to postpone an up close and very personal final encounter with my own mortal selfhood.

And, my caring family and friends who immeasurably enrich this continued adventure.

Larry Bell

Introduction

What happens after the stage lights dim and the curtains close? Does our personal life get an encore or sequel?

A most dispiriting reflection on this is offered by German philosopher Arthur Schopenhauer in *Perega and Paralipomena* (*Appendices and Omissions*):

> In early youth we sit before the impending course of our life like children at the theatre before the curtain is raised, who sit there in happy and excited expectation of the things that are to come. It is a blessing that we do not know what will actually come. For to the man who knows, the children may at times appear to be like innocent delinquents who are condemned not to death, it is true, but to life and have not yet grasped the purport of their sentence. Nevertheless everyone wants to reach old age and thus to a state of life, whereof it may be said: 'It is bad today and every day it will get worse, until the world of all happens.'

Schopenhauer's grim view of life's theater is far different than my own. First, life always seems preferable to the alternative. Second, the next world he awaits has always been here, and always will be. The show will go on, and that's a good thing. At least that's how I see it.

Why I Wrote this Book

This manuscript of musings has been in my mind-works for most of a lifetime, dating back to my earliest remembered thoughts. It reflects a personal quest to understand how my life—all life—fits into some larger natural order.

I first became motivated to put some of these ideas in writing in a non-published set of 100 essays titled *Reflections on Oceans and Puddles*[1] (big things and little things) that I wrote for my two sons when they were very young. From my perspective, it was not intended to imply that "bigger" subjects are most important in any fundamental ways. Marvels revealed by the inner workings of a cell or atom are not necessarily any less significant than those associated with the outer workings of the Universe. Nor is a concept of *God* that is contemplated through elaborate religious and philosophical discourses more profound than one recognized in the elegant beauty of a flower or a kind and unselfish act.

During my childhood and youth people around me seldom, if ever, talked about religion. Most of us attended one church or another. Almost everyone I knew was Christian, and being cursed with more than an ordinary share of curiosity, I found it impossible to escape questions concerning many aspects of theology. Since I was unaware that anyone else, except for maybe some evil people, had similar uncertainties, I arranged a meeting to discuss this dilemma with my minister.

In particular, I wondered why a God who was so great as to be able to create a Universe would really care if humans worshiped Him. And why would a loving God create a hell for those who didn't? Instead, wouldn't a God who blessed us with natural curiosity and intelligence intend us to guiltlessly use those gifts?

---

[1] The Author, *Reflections on Oceans and Puddles: One Hundred Reasons to be Very Grateful, Enthusiastic and Hopeful*

My pastor, a kind and thoughtful man, admitted that he also had similar questions—but asked me to please not mention this to anyone else. I regretted having lived with that private guilt for so long after he suggested that I consider a life in the ministry.

While I do generally consider myself to be a religious person, there is no single faith I subscribe to. Rather, I respect fundamental principles attached to many.

It may be useful to remember that the most ancient Jewish scriptures are steeped in democratic ideals and incorporate concern for moral aid and tolerance among all people. These concepts have had powerful influences upon other religions, including Christianity and Islam.

Mohammad and Buddha preached that there is no separation between the physical and spiritual world. The *Quran* instructs us to observe God's creation, work to understand those natural systems, and constantly endeavor to seek knowledge.

Secular lessons have also advanced our understanding of natural and moral principles. Aristotle, Plato and Socrates are credited with establishing the foundations for modern philosophy and ethical reasoning in ancient Greece which later influenced the thinking of Saint Thomas Aquinas in the 13th century, and Charles Darwin in the 20th.

Prevailing religious orthodoxies have not always embraced scientific discoveries. Galileo defended his belief that our Earth revolves around the Sun in the face of 17th century charges of heresy by leaders of the Roman Catholic Church. That concept displaced man from the center of the Universe. Johannes Kepler, a devout Protestant, was similarly ostracized by members of his church after he calculated the motion of the Earth and other planets around a stationary Sun; a heretical notion at the time which now makes space travel possible.

Albert Einstein, who exemplified high intellectual achievement and moral consciousness put it this way:

The further the spiritual evolution of mankind advances, the more certain it seems to me that the path to genuine religiosity does not lie through the fear of life, and the fear of death, and blind faith, but through striving after rational knowledge.[2]

Being Part of Something Really Big

Looking at our Earth home in a remote suburb of the Milky Way amongst billions of other galaxies we can imagine ourselves as either insignificantly tiny or part of something unimaginably marvelous and immense.

My earliest memory of self-revelation is when I was a child, probably about seven or eight years old, sitting quietly alone outside my house. The long Wisconsin winter had retreated, and grass began to appear amidst remaining patches of melting snow. The Sun was warm on my back, and the musky fragrance of wet earth was strong.

It suddenly dawned on me that I was directly connected to that magical world of my backyard. The materials that comprised the soil, grass, trees and even stones were the same stuff I was made of. I wasn't just a spectator experiencing nature. I was actually part of nature, and somehow always would be, long after the trees were gone. That awareness was very exciting to me then, and continues to be now.

We are truly creatures of the natural Universe. The elements that constitute every part of us and our beautiful blue planet passed through other fiery stars, now gone, long before our mother Sun was born. Each of those elements, in turn, are comprised of atoms

---

[2] Albert Einstein, *Out of My Later Years,* Wing Books, New York, Avenel, New Jersey, Copyright 1956 by the Estate of Albert Einstein, published 1993 and distributed by Outlook Book company, Inc., a Random House company.

which are like tiny solar systems containing tremendous energy, each with a proton and neutron nucleus orbited by electrons that together direct the complex chemistry of life.

That Universe that spawned us is unimaginably vast and marvelous. Consider, if you will, that there are estimated to be more than 100 billion stars in our Milky Way galaxy, most which are larger than our "yellow dwarf" Sun. This spiral wheel is about 100,000 light years in diameter.

If we were somehow able to travel to a new star in our galaxy every hour of the day and night, it would take about six million years, much longer than humans have existed, to visit only about half of them.

Now also consider that there are estimated to be more than 100 billion galaxies in our known Universe. The Universe which has existed about 13.7 billion years, about 9 billion years longer than our home planet, is constantly changing, like a garden where new plants bud as others wither on a cosmic time schedule.

From our vantage point on a spiral arm of our galaxy, it is difficult to grasp the reality that those distant stars, and the planets and ghostly clouds that surround them, are part of our personal world. Humankind has a history of resisting any observations that placed us outside the center of the Universe. And in reality, the Universe probably has no center, except maybe a theoretical point where a Big Bang first set everything in motion. Yet there is really nothing to be upset about. The real estate we occupy has a wonderful location suited perfectly to our lives and a spectacular view.

Another difficulty many people seem to have with a cosmic perspective is that they feel it diminishes their significance. Perhaps you have seen graphic illustrations depicting the Milky Way galaxy, possibly printed on a tee shirt, with an arrow pointing to our solar system neighborhood with a note stating "you are here". Some will take this as evidence that we are indeed small-timers living in the celestial boondocks. Others, however, may interpret this very differently, recognizing that we are all an integral part of something unfathomably majestic and empowering.

Yes, while it is true that our community and bodies are small relative to the Universe, we should remember that everything is small relative to the Universe. After all, does size really have anything at all to do with importance? Are boulders more important than hamsters? Is Saturn more important than the Earth? It seems to me that either everything is important, or nothing is. And that is purely a matter of personal decision.

The idea of a changing Universe can also be disquieting for some. If even planets, stars and galaxies are constantly being born and changing, ultimately only to die, then where does our human destiny lie? Upon what permanent ground can we build our spiritual refuge?

One answer is that change is the essential nature of life and spirit. Everything that we have the good judgment to enjoy is dynamic, revealing new dimensions of possibility with each transformation and discovery. The exciting news, if we accept it, is that nature is eternal, or as close to that as we dare imagine. And as manifestations of that wonderful condition, we are too.

We are here

Larry Bell

Part of Something Really, Really Big

Our home located in a remote spiral arm of but one among an estimated 350 million large galaxies is perceived by some as a humbling reality. Add to that an estimate that Earth's Solar System is only one of an estimated 400 billion stars inhabiting our Milky Way galaxy alone, with the visible Universe containing 30 billion trillion (2×10^{22}) more.

Yes, we are indeed very tiny compared to the Universe...just as everything is small relative to the Universe. We can only wonder then how we got so lucky to be part of this unfathomably majestic miracle.

7

Are We Alone Out "Here"?

I believe alien life is quite common in the Universe, although intelligent life is less so. Some say it has yet to appear on planet Earth.
—Stephen Hawking

So first, let's assume that by "intelligent" life we're referring to creatures we might be able to engage in meaningful communications if not actually enjoy socializing with; particularly if they don't pose a threat to self-esteem and wellbeing. Well according to a famous "Drake equation", the probable number of such communicating civilizations could be quite enormous.

Formulated by Frank Drake in 1961, the Drake equation speculates probabilities regarding the number of planetary civilizations by factoring in such considerations as: the rate of star formation; the fraction of those stars with habitable planets; the fraction of those planets which might develop life; the fraction of intelligent life; the further fraction of those capable of developing detectable technology; and finally, the length of time such civilizations might be detectable. The fundamental problem here is that sound statistical estimates are rendered impossible since our own circumstances offer the only known (and highly biased) example.

Those estimates vary widely. In 1966 Carl Sagan optimistically suggested that there might be as many as one million communicating civilizations in the Milky Way alone, although he later decided that number might be far smaller. Mathematical physicists Frank Tipler and John D. Barrow—far more pessimistically—put their average-per-galaxy guess at less than one.

In any case, more than 50 years of SETI radio telescope searches haven't turned up any signs of intelligent alien presence yet...no evidence that our galaxy is teeming with powerful transmitters other than our own continuously broadcasting and receiving near the 21cm hydrogen frequency as we hoped to find.

Frank Drake described his own equation as just a way of "organizing our ignorance" on the subject. Still, as a general roadmap of what we need to learn in order to understand this existential question, it has formed the backbone of astrobiology as a science.

According to a "Fermi-Hart paradox", it looks like the odds of finding intelligent life on other Earth-like planets aren't great due to the long time required for such beings to evolve coupled with a relatively short remaining life span of our planet when the Sun brightens as predicted in another billion years or so. Physicists Enrico Fermi and Michael Hart argued given that our Sun is a typical and relatively young star while billions of stars in the galaxy are billions of years older, we should have seen some evidence of advanced alien civilizations by now.

Hence Fermi's question: Where is everybody?

If We Have Company, Are they Impressed?

Okay, before I go any farther on this, let me be clear that I don't have a clue whether or not our planet has previously been visited by aliens, they are currently watching and studying us, or as really advanced intellects who already know pretty much everything even find us worth all the trouble. But just for fun, just as author John Updike did in his 1968 short story *Bech Takes Pot Luck,* let's imagine what they might find.

The lead character here, Henry Bech, a Jewish American novelist struggling for fame, is invited to give a reading at a Virginia all-girl college where he is regarded as a literary star. Upon arriving he experiences a crisis of faith not only in himself as an author, but in the value of human art itself.

At a dinner in his honor, he:

...saw that even in an age of science and unbelief our ideas are dreams, styles, superstitions, mere animal noises intended to repel or attract. He looked around the ring of munching females and saw their bodies as a Martian or mollusk might see them, as pulpy stalks of bundled nerves oddly pinched to a bud of concentration in the head, a hairy bone knob holding some pounds of jelly in which trillions of circuits, mostly dead, kept records, coded motor operations, and generated an excess of electricity that pressed into the hairless side of the head and leaked through the orifices, in the form of pained, hopeful noises and a simian dance of wrinkles. Impossible mirage! A blot on nothingness.

Bech concluded:

...the void should have been left unvexed; should have been spared this trouble of matter of life, and, worst, of consciousness.

Contemplating God

I believe in Spinoza's God who reveals himself in orderly harmony of what exists, not in a God who concerns himself with the fares and actions of human beings.
—Albert Einstein (1961) responding to a New York rabbi who asked him if he believed in God.[3]

Dutch philosopher Baruch Spinoza (1632-1677) came to be regarded as one of Western philosophy's most influential thinkers. Laying the groundwork for modern conceptions of "self" and the

[3]*Einstein for the 21ˢᵗ Century,* ed. Peter Galison et al., Princeton University Press, 2008, p.37

Universe. Those highly controversial ideas which challenged tenants of the Hebrew Bible and nature of the Divine led to his expulsion by religious authorities from Jewish society by age 23, and the inclusion of his writings on the Catholic Church's *Index of Forbidden Books*.

Spinoza perceived God and Nature as one. He wrote:

> *Whether we say…that all things happen according to the laws*
> *of nature, or are ordered by the decree and direction of God,*
> *we say the same thing.*

Both comprise a whole, infinite, eternal, necessarily existing, active system of the Universe within which absolutely everything exists.

Contending "Deus sive Natura" (God is Nature), Spinoza envisioned a God that does not rule over the Universe through Province in which a Deity can make changes, but rather a God which itself is a deterministic system by which:

> *things could not have been produced by God in any other way*
> *or in any other order than is the case.*

This directly challenged a transcendental view of a God which actively responds to events in the Universe. Everything that has or will happen is part of a long chain of metaphysical cause and effect events which humans are unable to change through any amount of prayer.

Spinoza regarded intellectual love of reality to be the highest end for humans. Since God could not possibly stand apart from nature, it follows that the Universe is divine: eternal, infinite and the cause of its own existence…hence worthy of our awe and reverence.

That God Question

Although clearly no Einstein, I too have been asked if I believe in "God". The easiest response would be to say yes, and simply let it go at that. Not wishing to offend those whose concepts of a Supreme Deity are based upon very specific religious doctrine, that answer would be partly true.

For example, many of us might agree that God is love, God is good, and as Spinoza foresaw, God is Nature. By accepting all three facts, then we, as incarnations of Nature are ideally imbued with God's love and goodness...no argument there.

My problems arise when people who ask assume a common agreement that any answer applies a homo-centric Man-God definition which rather narrow-mindedly envisions a world created primarily for people. If God had that in mind, it seems unlikely that the Creator would have bothered to make the Universe so timeless and vast. It would be like building a whole planet and nation of cities to accommodate transient residents of a single planetary household.

If God created planet Earth most exclusively for human purposes, I am perplexed by the fact that the Great Architect invested so much creativity making such an incredible menagerie of creatures, large and small, which seem to have little or no connection to our lives and well-being. These include countless microorganisms, insects, reptiles, birds and animals of endless variation that would probably be far more content if we had never arrived on the scene.

And let's not forget the astounding variety of dinosaurs that roamed our planet for millions of years, long before the first human child clutched an acorn toy. If Nature God had an intelligent purpose for creating Homo sapiens, then wouldn't the same logically apply to them as well?

Regardless of religious and philosophical orientations, if people truly recognize themselves to be reflections of God's natural love and goodness, it is difficult to comprehend cruel travesties that have been justified in God's name. How many senseless wars and acts of fiendish brutality have been perpetrated under the guise of divine guidance? History has taught us that when neighbors in dispute claim to have God on their side, it's probably a very good idea to get women and children inside the house and lock livestock in the barn.

Also, when anyone tells us that God has given them a message which we must either believe or suffer eternal damnation, perhaps we might legitimately question the authenticity of those spiritual channels. They are either quite misguided in failing to recognize God's loving Nature, or are attempting to manipulate us through fear…maybe even both. In any event, it isn't nice.

Contemplating what God is and isn't has led me along different paths, always producing more questions than answers. No single religion yet encountered has satisfied my curiosity about God's true Nature or Nature's true God. Admittedly, since there are reportedly more than a thousand separate religious groups registered in America alone, I have doubtless overlooked a few possibilities.

I once naively expected that quests for such lofty answers motivated most scientists…physicists in particular. Any such assumption was dashed when as a freshman student taking a university physics class I became excited about some now-forgotten metaphysical implications of Michael Faraday's 19th century ballistic cannon experiments. Accordingly, I arranged an appointment with a Nobel laureate physicist in the department.

He listened attentively with only slight traces of amusement as I discussed the great significance of my observation at length. When I had finished, he gently told me that he really never thought about such momentous matters. He then explained that he just enjoyed solving puzzles.

I later concluded that he had shared an important lesson with me after all. Maybe the perplexities associated with Nature and God should be regarded as special challenges that make life more interesting and fun. Perhaps that is exactly what the Creator had in mind.

Inflation: 10-36sec.
Atom Nuclei: 3min.
1st Atoms:300K yrs.
Galaxies: 10-15B yrs.
(Earth Solar System about 4.7B yrs. ago)

Emergence of Homo Sapien 130K Years Ago

Larry Bell

Time Elapsed since the Big Bang

The Universe we inhabit is a living space. Like a garden, stars and planets blossom, only to die and be replaced on clock-less schedules.

Our family ancestors are late comers on this cosmic landscape. Anatomically modern humans have only existed over about the past 130,000 years, compared with a great variety of dinosaurs that arrived approximately 231 million years earlier and survived over 135 million more until about 66 million years ago.

Who/What Made God?

If you postulate a "creative force", then you must be prepared to postulate one before that to explain its existence...and another before that.
—Jim Holt, Author of *Why Does the World Exist?*[4]

Stephen Hawking begins his book *A Brief History of Time* with an anecdote he attributes to Bertrand Russell. As reported, during a public lecture on cosmology Russell was interrupted by an old lady in the audience who told him that everything he said was rubbish...she purportedly said:

The world is actually flat, and it's supported by a giant elephant that is standing on the back of a giant turtle.

When Russell asked what was supporting the turtle, she replied:

But it's turtles all the way down.

And perhaps very fertile turtles at that. After all, the word "cosmology" derives from Greek "kosmos" (Universe) and "gonos" (produce)... the same as "gonad". Cosmos and cosmetic also have the same Greek root for "adornment" or "arrangement".

But then again, who/what created all those turtles, the first reproducing pair at the infinite "bottom", in particular? Most scientists seem to believe that that epic mating scene began with a very big bang indeed.

In 1965, two Bell Laboratory scientists in New Jersey detected a "hiss" that turned out to be what is believed to be a microwave

---

[4] Jim Holt, *Why Does the World Exist?*, 2012, Liveright Publishing Company, A Division of W.W. Norton & Company, New York-London, p140-142

echo caused by photons left over from a "Big Bang" of a beginning. If you tune your television between stations, about 10 percent of those black-and-white specks you see are remnants of that afterglow.

The Big Bang theory gradually won the popular endorsement of scientists as a plausible explanation of how the early Universe expanded, cooled and congealed from a primordial soup into stars, planets and galaxies.

Conditions had to be spectacularly right for that theory to play out. Princeton Professor Robert Dicke's "flatness problem" predicts the mass density and expansion rate for the Universe which has been expanding for nearly 14 billion years must be exquisitely balanced for it to look anything like it is today. At one second after the Big Bang this balance must have been within 15 decimal places of one, lying in the miniscule interval between 0.999999999999 and 1.000000000000001.[5]

If that perfect balance weren't present, another series of "grand unified theories" predicted that the existence of "magnetic monopoles" would have caused the early Universe to collapse. These are magnets with isolated North or South poles rather than normal equal-strength North-South poles.

Also, as MIT Professor Alan Guth points out:

> *The Big Bang theory says nothing about what banged, why it banged, or what happened before it banged.*[6]

---

[5] Alan P. Lightman, *Ancient Light: Our Changing View of the Universe,* January 1, 1993, Harvard University Press ISBN 978-0-674-03363-4
[6] Alan Guth, *What made the Big Bang bang,* Neil Swidley, May 2, 2014, Boston Globe Magazine
http://www.bostonglobe.com/magazine/2014/05/02/alan-guth-what-made-big-bang-bang/RmI4s9yCI56jKF6ddMiF4L/story.html

As for the "what" question, a whole lot less than we might possibly imagine.

A "chaotic inflation" theory advanced by Guth and Andrei Linde, a Moscow physicist who is now at Stanford, postulates that all that is needed to create a Universe is a hundred-thousandth of a gram of matter. That's enough to create a small chunk of vacuum that blows up into billions and billions of galaxies. It follows from this that all physical matter in the Universe gets created from negative energy in the gravitational field.

The chaotic inflation theory got a big boost on March 17, 2014 when a team of radio astronomers led by John Kovac at the Harvard-Smithsonian Center for Astrophysics in Cambridge, Massachusetts found the imprint of gravitational waves from the Big Bang mapped from a telescope at the Earth's South Pole. These vortex-like, or curly patterns are believed to be a tell-tale sign of expansion just 380,000 years after the Universe banged onto the scene.

In his book *Why Does the World Exist?*, Jim Holt asks:

> How can a chunk of vacuum (essentially nothing but empty space) really create something?

Well, as he notes, maybe this can be explained by a "quantum vacuum" theory proposed by Edward Tryon at the Department of Physics and Astronomy, Hunter College of the City University of New York.

In a 1973 paper published in the British science journal *Nature* titled *Is the Universe a Vacuum Fluctuation?*, Tryon proposes that consistent with quantum field theory that empty space really isn't empty after all. Instead, it can be conceptualized as a mathematical structure that bends and flexes like rubber. Saturated with electromagnetic energy fields and seething with virtual-particle activity it's a Universe that can pop in and out of existence. Tyron concludes:

In answer to the question why it happened, I offer the modest proposal that our Universe is simply one of those things which happens from time to time.[7]

Perhaps that happens when the Creator gets bored.

---

[7] Edward P. Tryon, *Is the Universe a Vacuum Fluctuation?*, December 14,1973, Nature 246, 396-397, Department of Physics and Astronomy, Hunter College of the City University of New York, New York, New York 10021

Larry Bell

It's Turtles all the Way Down

Inquisitive minds might ponder what Genesis force and sequence of events caused the birth of the Universe with a Big Bang between 10-15 billion years ago.

Larry Bell

/Quantum Theory Shrinks Reality

The general theory of relativity which governs cosmic evolution at the largest scale breaks down when "things" really get small. First published by Albert Einstein in 1916, it generalized special relativity and Newton's law of universal gravitation, providing a unified description of gravity as a geometric property of space and time (or "spacetime"). Here, spacetime curves according to the energy and momentum of whatever matter and radiation are present. This relationship is specified by Einstein's field equations, a system of partial differential equations.

At the moment of the Big Bang, the boundary of spacetime, the equations of relativity break down and classical physics no longer applied. A tiny fraction of a second later the entire "observable" Universe was no bigger than an atom, and temperature, density and curvature of the Universe all go to infinity.

Alexander Vilenkin, who directs the Institute of Cosmology at Tufts University, visualizes spacetime like the closed surface of a sphere which curves back on itself until the radius goes all the way to zero. That's when it can get interesting. Using principles of quantum theory, a tiny bit of that energy-filled vacuum could then spontaneously "tunnel" into existence...like maybe one hundred-trillionth of a centimeter. Driven by negative pressure of inflation it could undergo runaway expansion...attaining cosmic proportions in microseconds...a cascading fireball of light and matter...the Big Bang.

In 1970 physicists Stephen Hawking and Robert Penrose proceeded to prove with mathematical certainty that the Universe must have begun as a "singularity". Hawking foresaw that quantum theory previously used to describe subatomic phenomena could then be applied to the Universe as a whole...the concept of quantum cosmology.

But quantum theory has big limitations too. Most particularly, it "forbids" a sharply defined state of affairs, decreeing that nature at the most fundamental level is irredeemably fuzzy. It does, however, allow particles to spontaneously pop out of a vacuum. In other words, according to quantum mechanics, "nothingness" is an unstable state of affairs.

"Heisenberg's uncertainty principle" states that certain pairs of properties which are called "canonically conjugate variables" are linked in such a manner that they can't both be precisely measured simultaneously. One such pair is the value of a field and the rate its field value changes. It follows then that since nothingness by definition is a state in which all field values are equal to zero, any mathematical description of changeless emptiness is incompatible with quantum mechanics...making nothingness unstable.

Another pair is position and momentum. The more precisely you locate the position of a subatomic particle, the less you know about its momentum and vice versa. The same applies to indeterminate calculations of a time and energy pairing.

So it seems that the more we know about one thing, the less we know about something else. Sounds to me like a pretty good characterization of academia.

My Place in the Natural Scheme

How can I, who am thinking about the entire, centerless Universe, be anything so specific as THIS, this measly, gratuitous creature, existing in a tiny morsel of spacetime, with a definite and by no means universal mental and physical organization? How can I be anything so small and concrete and specific?
—Thomas Nagel, *The View from Nowhere*

It seems quite natural to me that we tend to view ourselves not only as integral parts of the vast Universe, but from a personal vantage point where it seems that everything revolves around us. I expect that this self-centric world perspective originates long before we ever leave the womb. As a fetus we begin to experience ourselves through consciousness of our mother's sudden movements and heartbeats which are amplified by the protective sea that surrounds us.

After birth we are flooded with new experiences. The familiar and comforting heartbeats are replaced my louder, more varied sounds, including our own voices. Blurry objects appear in our new field of vision including our own hands and feet. We encounter other sensations for the first time, including tastes, smells and temperature changes. Some are uncomfortable, such as hunger and stomach gas. And we learn how to communicate displeasure with our lungs, facial muscles and tears to summon help.

It takes a while to differentiate ourselves from other objects and events around us to know boundaries where we end and everything else begins. Yet we soon discover that those things which are uniquely part of us can be directly controlled or experienced through our senses. For example, we can move and make sounds on our own command. We can open our eyes to see, or close them to shut light out.

We can feel things that touch us, but not things that touch someone else. We begin to recognize ourselves as distinctly "us" separate from "them". As the center of our own world we feel very special; so special, in fact, that everyone and everything outside ourselves seems to have been put there for our benefit.

And while humbling experiences in that vast outside world later teach us that this assumption is far from accurate, that's quite okay. They should also make us feel even more special and grateful to be part of it.

Being a Natural Born Winner

If you tend to be somewhat complacent about life, you might consider that you were born against incredible odds. Let's take just a few moments to review some statistics.

Your mother came into this world with about one million ova, of which only about 400 of these could have been expected to ever fully mature into eggs. Of those eggs most waited decades for an opportunity to experience fertile fulfillment, only to be swept away in red floods.

Your father's contenders for self-actualization had chances which were even far worse. Assuming that your dad was typical, he produced about 200 million sperm cells every day until numbers began to taper off at about the age of 45. If you were conceived when he was about 30 years old, we might imagine that about 1.5 trillion of those unfortunate little tadpoles fell by the wayside before they could enter anyone's gene pool.

When your opportunity as a sperm carrying half of your genetic identity came along, you faced awesome competition. There you were among 3,000 million or so would-be half-brothers and sisters waiting in the win-or-die Ovarian Marathon. Timing for all contestants was critical. What if the egg wasn't waiting? What if one of your parents was away on a trip somewhere? What if your mother had a headache?

Of course the results are now history. The race wasn't cancelled after all. Released with a mighty surge, you swam with heroic determination and were first to reach the finish line which hardened around you as a barrier to all others. You then shared your genetic treasures to begin a whole new life.

As remarkable as that victory was, it reveals only one episode among countless events of unbelievably good fortune that supported your success.

What if your father and mother had never met? Recognizing that the United States population alone is about 320 million people, they both had many other mates to choose from. Not only did their lives have to intersect at the same place and time, all conditions in their personal circumstances had to be compatible for that relationship to occur.

Similar coincidences (or divinely orchestrated plans) had to also occur in the lives of your grandparents. Your birth, in fact, depended upon a unique and unbroken chain of events involving ancestors dating back over the history of our human species. Conservatively assuming that this amounts to about 100 billion people so far, that's a fantastically lucky lottery ticket.

Those improbable events leading up to your birth may have limited meaning to those whose lives are not directly connected to your own. Beyond your spouse, your children, and their children, ad-infinitum, most everyone else's life would probably go on pretty much in the same general way if you hadn't been born. If you hadn't arrived, no one would know the difference.

On the other hand, being born is the opportunity of your lifetime! It is an opportunity to let people appreciate what they would be missing without you. It is an opportunity to make good use of that genetic potential that you have won to experience life as fully as possible.

You might remind yourself that being only one person in a general population of billions does not make you or them less special. This is easiest to remember when we put ourselves in the company of people who recognize they are born winners too. In accepting their own importance they are likely to respect your value as well.

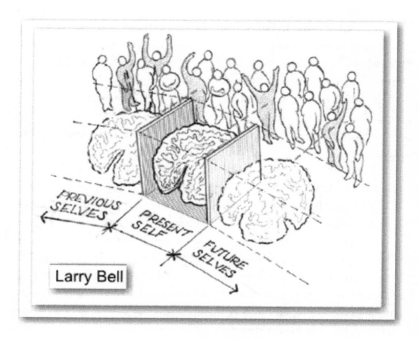

Larry Bell

Eternal Mind in a Box Thought Experiment

One aspect of tunnel vision is our inability to see before and beyond present lifetimes.

Imagine this tiny bit of space-time you currently occupy as merely a random microsecond sampling of eternity. Also visualize your self-aware "mind" in a box suspended in that cosmic continuum with a window now open only to the present. Is it logical to believe this sensate existence to be but a singular one-time event?

But just who is really Me?

American psychologist and humanist philosopher Carl Rogers described self-concept as:

> ...*the organized consistent conceptual gestalt composed of perceptions of the characteristics of 'I' or 'me' and the perceptions of the relationships of the 'I' or 'me' to others and to various aspects of life, together with the values attached to these perceptions. It is a gestalt which is available to awareness though not necessarily in awareness. It is a fluid and changing gestalt, a process, but at any given moment it is a specific entity.*[8]

However, as Austrian-born philosopher Ludwig Wittgenstein observed, just as the eye which is the source of the visual field but not in that visual field cannot see itself, so it is with the "I" which is the source of our consciousness.

This condition is analogous to a Geico insurance commercial where we see a gecko lizard character walking through a stone tunnel towards an opening. When he approaches it we witness him looking out searching for Mount Rushmore from the entrance connection in George Washington's eye which he was unaware of from inside.

So it often is with self-perception.

Post-Cartesian philosophy laid down two broad conceptual requirements that "self" must meet. First it must embody consciousness awareness...experiences at a particular moment gained through the senses. The second is being capable of self-

---

[8] *Rogers, Carl. (1959), A Theory of Therapy, Personality Relationships as Developed in the Client-Centered Framework.* In (Ed.) S. Koch. *Psychology: A Study of a Science. Vol. 3: Formulations of the person and the social context.* New York: McGraw Hill.

consciousness, an awareness of "me-ish" experience that sets one independently apart from everyone else.

My interpretation of self-perception can be visualized in an abstract "brain in a box" thought experiment. Imagine, if you will, that you are a conscious mind wired with sensory connections in a closed container floating in spacetime. Suddenly a door in the box opens, and you can see unfamiliar figures outside. All but one are eating candy bars (which you also don't comprehend), and you watch them unimpressed.

As the other one then begins to eat, you immediately taste the sweet chocolate. Now you become interested in that figure, and through continued involvement with it, additional experiences are opened to you. You also learn that you can command that particular individual do marvelous things, and accept it as being yourself.

Oh, and there's one other lesson in this. Now imagine that this moment when the door opens to your experience, is but a random sample of the eternal spacetime continuum. What if the door opened to another moment a few eons ago, or a few eons in the future? Wouldn't you expect to experience contact with a figure that is attached to your awareness then also?

Jim Holt offers some interesting thought experiments in his book *Why Does the World Exist?* First regarding whether genetic identity really defines an individual he asks us to imagine that you were born an identical twin, but the zygote that split apart shortly after fertilization to produce you and your twin had instead remained a single clump of cells.

> *Would the unique baby born to your parents nine months later have been you? Your twin? Neither?*

Then there's that self we inhabit or possess which comprises psychological criterion of identity, the "I" whose existence is determined by a more or less continuous and distinctive bundle of memories, perceptions, thoughts and intentions. Holt asks:

But what happens if I undergo amnesia and lose all my memories? Or what if a fiendish neurosurgeon manages to erase all my memories and replace them with your memories? And what if he performed the reverse operation on you? Would we find ourselves waking up in each other's body?

Following up on that notion, Holt then asks us to consider a grim hypothetical scenario proposed in 1970 by the philosopher Bernard Williams if our answer was "yes":

"You are informed that you are going to be tortured tomorrow. Understandably, this makes you fearful. But prior to the torture, you are told, your memories will be wiped out by the fiendish neurosurgeon and replaced with my memories. Would you still have reason to fear the torture? If you did, it would mean that, despite your complete psychological makeover as me, it would still be you who endured the pain.[9]

Oxford Philosopher Derek Parfit offers still another grim hypothetical:

You are in a terrible accident. Your body is fatally injured, as are the brains of your two identical-triplet brothers. Your brain is divided into two halves, and into each brother's body one half is successfully transplanted. After the surgery, each of the two resulting people believes himself to be you, seems to remember living your life, and has your character. (This is not as unlikely as it sounds: already, living brains have been surgically divided, resulting in two separate streams of consciousness.) What has happened? Have you died, or have

---

[9] *Body Swapping, The Newsletter of the Philosophical Discussion Group of British Mensa*, Theo Todman, Commensal Issue No. 105, February 2001

you survived? And if you have survived who are you? Are you one of these people? Both? Or neither? What if one of the transplants fails, and only one person with half your brain survives? That seems quite different—but the death of one person could hardly make a difference to the identity of another. [10]

In other words, Parfit argues that since neither of the people is you, it really doesn't matter that you have ceased to exist, because what has happened to you is quite unlike ordinary death. Through your relationship with the two new people you have everything that matters in ordinary survival—a continuity of memories and dispositions that will decay and change as they usually do. Most of us care about our future because it is ours. Personal identity is not what truly matters.

---

[10] *How to Be Good*, Larissa Macfarquhar, The New Yorker, Annals of Ideas, September 5, 2011

Larry Bell

The Eye Cannot See Itself

*But by reflection, by some other things...And since
you cannot see yourself so well as by reflection, I,
your glass, will modestly discover to yourself that
of yourself which know not of.*
—**William Shakespeare,** *Julius Caesar*

**As with the gecko character in a GEICO insurance
commercial searching for Mount Rushmore, such
tunnel vision often obscures glaring realities in life that
surrounds us.**

31

Is it All in Our Minds?

I tend to think that self-awareness involving beings personally connected to each of us populates the span of eternity. If so, is this connection with our "mind", and what, specifically is that?

Some philosophers hold that mental phenomena are in some respects non-physical. Plato envisioned mind-body relationships for all living organisms which include a nutritive soul of growth and metabolism which migrates to a new physical body upon death. Aristotle further elaborated this into a hierarchical arrangement whereby animals and people share a perceptive soul of pain, pleasure and desire, but only people enjoy the faculty of reason. He believed that all of this dies when the organism perishes.

Plato's allegory *Phaedo* likens our understanding of the objects and phenomena by which we perceive the world to emerging from a dark cave into sunlight where only vague shadows of what lies beyond that prison are cast dimly upon the wall. Those shadow forms of perception are both non-physical and non-mental, existing nowhere in time, space, mind or matter.

Aristotle argued that in order for animals to perceive and for humans to reason, perfect copies rather than shadows of forms are required. He reasoned that the human mind can literally assume any form being contemplated or experienced, and is unique in its ability to become a blank state with no essential form.

Plato and Aristotle both influenced writings of Saint Thomas Aquinas during the early Middle Ages which have been integrated into Roman Catholic doctrine. Like Aristotle, Aquinas perceived the human being as a unified composite substance embodying two substantial principles: form and matter.

And while Aquinas believed that the intellectual soul is able to subsist upon death of a human being, he did not believe that the human person is able to remain integrated at death. This is because the separated intellectual soul is not a man. Accordingly, a pleading that "soul of St. Peter pray for us" is more appropriate than "St. Peter pray for us" since all things connected with this person, including memories, ended with his corporeal life.

During the mid-17th century, the dualism philosophy of Rene Descartes envisioned the mind as a nonphysical substance capable of consciousness and self-awareness separate from the brain as the seat of intelligence.

In his *Meditations on First Philosophy* Descartes determined that while he could doubt whether he had a body (it could be a dream or illusion created by an evil demon), he could not doubt that he had a mind. The mind was a "thinking thing" with the essence of himself which doubts, believes, hopes and contemplates. This led to his best known philosophical statement "Cogito ergo sum", or "I think, therefore I am".

A recurring question regarding Descartes' dualism premise is how an immaterial mind can cause physical events, and vice versa. Struggling for a feasible answer, he proposed that animal spirits may interact with the body through the small pineal gland located between the two brain hemispheres. Some of his disciples including Arnold Geulincx and Nicholas Malebranch suggested another possibility...where all mind-body interactions require direct intervention of God.

Surprisingly for many, Spinoza concluded in *Ethics* (EVP22ff) that:

> *The human mind cannot be absolutely destroyed with the body, but something of it remains which is eternal.*

This suggests that while the human mind has a temporal and non-temporal part, this eternal non-temporal something continues to be able to retrieve a temporal something following the brain's death. Furthermore, the non-temporal something of the human mind which is somehow able to be retained or retrieved by the physical temporal substance can grow expand during a human's lifetime.

In Advayavada Buddhism, Spinozism is viewed as a philosophy in which all reality is held to consist of only one substance, typically referred to as God or Nature, of which both material things and thought (e.g. body and mind) are matching attributes mirroring each other. Yet followers believe that what man and other sentient beings have in common with the rest of existence is not thought of any kind, but rather their "conatus".

This conatus is an innate striving or drive to persevere successfully in all sentient life, of which sentient cognition is but one element. From a human perspective, conatus is experienced in the form of "progress", which is similar to Te, the "virtuous power" of the Tao in Taoism.

Larry Bell

Plato's Cave Allegory

Plato's Socrates parable likens our limited understanding by which we perceive the world as analogous to prisoners chained in a cave since childhood whose sense of reality is shaped by watching shadows projected from flames onto a wall which they believe to be coming from outside.

They have no way to understand that those shadows are actually being cast by showmen carrying objects and puppets behind the wall they are chained to.

Larry Bell

Thought Experiment: Which Selves are You?

Derek Parfit's grim brain transfer thought experiment challenges us to ask what personal aspects most dominantly characterize our "true selves."

Is it your unique sensate awareness where you alone experience information from your nerve endings? Is it your deterministic ability to exert command and control prerogatives over personal thoughts and actions? Is it your personal memory which catalogs experiences in your life to guide values and decisions through lessons learned?

Our Defining Spiritual and Human Values

*Love the world as yourself, and you'll be able to care for it
properly.*
—*Taoism: Tao Te Ching, 13*

How does God want us to behave? That, of course depends a lot
upon who we ask.

Spinoza didn't think that the question is relevant because it is
wrong to think of God as possessing human qualities such as
intellect and will. Spinoza's God is an entirely impersonal power
which neither rewards nor punishes behavior. That job is left to
cultural societies.

By viewing a God which does not act according to human
reasons and purposes, Spinoza challenged a most fundamental
tenant of Western thought. He concludes Book One of *Ethics*
suggesting that many human beings:

> ...*consider all natural things as means to their own
> advantage...*

and because of this they believe in:

> ...*a ruler of nature, endowed with human freedom, who had
> taken care of all things for them, and made all things for their
> use.*[11]

In doing so, Spinoza observed that people ascribe their own
characters and mental states to this divine ruler, conceiving God as
angry, loving or vengeful:

---

[11] Spinoza, part 3: *What God is Not*, Claire Carlisle, The Guardian,
February 21, 2011

So it has happened that each person has thought up from his own temperament different ways of worshiping God, so that God might love him above all others, and direct the whole of nature according to the needs of his blind desire and insatiable greed.

This view was quite different from one proposed by Aristotle who envisioned a creator God who made the world according to a plan with a certain purpose, a philosophy more consistent with the biblical narrative of Genesis.

At the same time, it would be overly simplistic to dismiss Spinoza as merely an atheist or skeptical agnostic. Although critical of "superstition", he was sympathetic to some aspects of Jewish and Christian teachings, arguing that Jesus had a singularly direct and immediate understanding of God, The embodiment of truth, and a role model for all human beings. Spinoza described the ideal human life as one devoted to love of God.

Purposeful Living

Friedrich Nietzsche believed that values are relative and subjective, and that the exemplary human being must craft his/her own identity through self-realization without relying on anything transcending that life—such as either a God or a soul. From his point of view every person should live his or her life for the sake of living it, not because of an anticipated afterlife, a concept he rejected.

Nietzsche viewed opposing psychological capacities that exist in everyone as great forces which must be balanced in order to live correctly and to realize a full life. In his way of thinking, morality is a matter of reason and conscience, not one tied to any religious faith.

Immanuel Kant saw things quite differently, believing that there can be no morality without religion. He theorized that moral thought has objective categories, differentiating between moral reasoning about how a person should act which he referred to as the "practical reason", vs. "pure reason" about something that exists.

Kant's categorical imperatives were perceived as universal in nature because they were there before being experienced. Accordingly, a person is duty-bound to act in a certain manner. Here, the action was more important than the outcome.

Kant supported what is now referred to as "foundations of retribution" or ("just deserts"), meaning that a person who commits a crime should receive nothing more or less than the penalty called for. This idea prominently appears in most cultures and religions. Christians refer to it as the *Golden Rule*, namely to *"Do onto others as you would have them do onto us."* Another translation is to remember: *"What goes around, comes around".*

Is there a concrete list of universal moral values? Numerous attempts by philosophers and theologians over the years have produced a variety of possibilities.

Pope John II broadly characterized universal moral law as being written on the human heart. Two modern religions, the Baha'i faith and Unitarian Universalist Church strive to promote universality as a central tenet.

English novelist Aldous Huxley argued that there is a "perennial philosophy" or core of moral principles that exist in every time and place throughout history. Indian independence leader Mahatma Gandhi advocated self-suffering, nonviolence and a search for truth as universal values. American philosopher William James believed that love is a singular foundation principle of all ethics. Charles Darwin speculated that the desire for approval is a primary root of morality.

A "short list" compilation of universal values by Richard Kinner and Jerry Kernes in the Division of Psychology in Education at Arizona State University-Tempe along with Phoenix counselor Therese Dautheribes (2000), drew upon well-known texts and documents of major world religions. Included are Judaism (the

Tanaka), Christianity (the *New Testament*), Islam (the *Koran*), Hinduism (the *Upanishads* and the *Bhagavad Gita*), Confucianism (the *Analects of Confucius*), Taoism (the *Tao Te Ching of Lao Tzu*), and Buddhism (the *Dhammapada*).

The study also consulted with and reviewed materials of several secular organizations, including the American Atheists Inc. (*Atheist Aims and Purpose, Atheism Teaches That*, and *Introduction to American Atheists*), the American Humanist Association (*Humanist Manifesto I, 1933* and *Humanist Manifesto II, 1973*), and the United Nations (*The United Nations Declaration of human Rights, 1948*).[12]

Here's what they came up with:

1. Commitment to something greater than self:
   - To recognize the existence of and be committed to a Supreme Being, higher principle, transcendent purpose or meaning to one's existence.
   - To seek the Truth (or truths).
   - To seek Justice.

2. Self-respect, but with humility, self-discipline, and acceptance of personal responsibility:
   - To respect and care for oneself.
   - To not exalt oneself or overindulge—to show humility and avoid gluttony, greed, or other forms of selfishness and self-centeredness.
   - To act in accordance with one's conscience and to accept responsibility for one's behavior.

---

[12] *A Short List of Moral Values*, Richard T. Kinnier et al, Counseling and Values, October 2000, Vol.45

3. Respect and caring for others (i.e., the Golden Rule):

- To recognize the connectedness between all people.
- To serve humankind and to be helpful to individuals.
- To be caring, respectful, compassionate, tolerant, and forgiving of others.
- To not hurt others (e.g., do not murder, abuse, steal from, cheat or lie to others).

4. Caring for other living things and the environment.

Bringing this down now to a personal level, what comprises a well-lived life? I had a sobering occasion to contemplate this during a conversation with a very close family member who was then in hospice care. He was someone I regarded to have lived a highly successful and well-lived life, and wished to communicate my appreciation of what this meant.

I told him that if I one day find myself reviewing my own achievements in the face of known near-term terminal realities, three questions will emerge above all: 1) did I have any fun?; 2) did I do any good?; and 3) did I fill my life with passion?

With regard to the first, in light of the apparently incredible genetic odds stacked against our arrivals on the scene, it would seem a terrible waste not to celebrate opportunities to enjoy it.

"Joie de vivre" (joy of living), a French phrase often used to express this priority, is characterized by Robert's Dictionary as "*sentiment exaltant ressenti par toute la conscience*", a sentiment that involves one's whole being. Psychologist Abraham Carl Rogers recognized a sense of playfulness - fun, joy, and amusement - to represent an important part of a self-actualized personality:

the quiet joy in being one's self...a spontaneous relaxed enjoyment, a primitive joie de vivre. [13]

In my view, doing "good" in summarizing one's life simply prompts each of us to ask whether or not we have attempted in good faith to respect the list of "universal values" which were previously outlined. It doesn't really have anything to do with having achieved wealth or fame, but rather asks us to contemplate: can I be trusted to be a good spouse, parent and friend?; do I have a generous nature where it comes to sharing credit and effort which recognizes the worth and contributions of others?; have I touched the lives of others in a constructive way simply because I could?; am I comfortable with that person that inhabits my own skin?

That third item...the "passion" word, is what to me sets humans apart from other perfectly wonderful creatures. Some might just as readily refer to this as "love". It should be apparent watching puppies and kittens at play that experiencing *joie de vivre* is not by any means unique to humans. As for "doing good", Darwin's theory attributing pursuit of reward or approval as a primary motive isn't entirely unique to our species either.

I believe that passion ratchets things up to a whole other level. It is what drives us to express our highest human potentials: to have empathy and truly care about others, to set goals, to meet challenges and seek excellence that set exceptional examples, to create music, art and literature that lifts our intellect and spirits, and to believe in the power of worthwhile ideas and our God-given abilities to make them real. A well-lived life requires no less.

---

[13] Rogers, Carl R, (1961). *On Becoming a Person: a Therapist's View of Psychotherapy*, Boston, MA, USA: Houghton Mifflin.

A Letter from a Japanese Father to His Son

My dear friend Itaru Tanaka was an exceptionally fine man who had a well-lived full, fascinating and distinguished life. His exposure as a child to death, suffering and destruction in Tokyo during World War II undoubtedly helped to shape his strong values, discipline and character. His career following graduation from Tokyo University as a well-known war correspondent, president of the Japan Press Club and companion-biographer of world leaders contributed to Itaru's insightful international and human perspective. Cancer ended his life in 1994.

A few years before Itaru's death, his son Makoto came to the U.S. to live with my family and attend the University of Houston. Nancy and I later discovered a letter he wrote to prepare Makoto for that adventure that I will now share with you. I'm very certain he wouldn't mind.

May 1989
Dear Makoto:
You may find it helpful for me to set forth our aims for your visit so that you can refer to them. I hope you will promise to keep a daily record of your experiences, however short those memories may be. It will be useful if you will include dates, times, and places.

I am making it materially possible for you to go to the New World so that you may gain first-hand experience managing your life outside the discipline imposed by school and family, and so that you may have a long and meaningful stay. This will enable you to gain direct knowledge about one of the largest, richest and most powerful countries in the world. Your life and career will be greatly influenced by this important experience.

Herein are some hints you may find useful in making a great success of your stay:

Getting the Most Out of Your Experience:

1. You must meticulously plan your days throughout the entire program. This is not only because good planning means good discipline. But also to enable you to get the most out of time available. Another cardinal principle which will be useful to you, not only during your visit, but always, is that living a good life requires that you do nothing in excess.

2. Be genuinely interested in people. Remember every person—be they young or old—has unique lessons to offer. Encourage them to talk about themselves and their families. When conversation lags you can always ask a sympathetic question or offer a thought-provoking statement.

Remember that a listener is always more appreciated than a talker and avoid boasting. On the other hand, don't fall into the other extreme of being too self-effacing or frightened to contribute to a conversation. Since I know that you do not suffer this problem, I find no reason to stress it.

3. Making friends involves being genuinely interested in people, their problems and their experiences; avoiding selfish and provocative acts; offering consideration and helpfulness; and being clean and well turned-out.

The best way to have a good time when you are with a group is to make sure that everybody participates and enjoys themselves. Don't be selfish in not caring what happens to others present so long as you are all right.

4. A great deal of experience in life can be obtained by closely observing the behavior and reactions of others, measuring their conduct against your own, and determining what standards you should apply. If the group you are with engages in bad practices, either in drink, sex or other matters, there is no need for you to go along with that behavior. If some members ridicule you about this, tell them that you gave a pledge to Professor and Mrs. Bell as well as to your parents, and insist that you intend to stick to that promise.

Observing the U.S.A.:

1. You will be living with an American family, reading their newspapers and watching their TV. You will find that many people are extremely ignorant about Japan, just as you and your father are ignorant about other countries. When you hear criticism about Japan and the Japanese people, avoid getting into heated arguments, but carefully listen and consider what they say.

Read newspapers and other publications available in the English language. Mark in pencil any word or expression that is unfamiliar and check it in the dictionary.

2. Try to meet people of all ages and backgrounds. Get involved in sports activities and youth clubs both off and on the university campus.

3. Make a point to learn something about U.S. History. This is absolutely essential to understand America's political actions and motivations, at home and abroad.

4. When you ask questions about the United States, keep the following in mind: "I am interested in how its people live, their expectations for the future, and what they expect regarding my appropriate behavior."

Personal Behavior:

1. Adjust to your host's lifestyle. Express your gratitude when you are kindly treated. It may be a good idea to give them flowers when you meet and leave them, or have them delivered by a florist. The value of the flowers might be between $5 and $10, or you may purchase an equivalent value in chocolates. In addition, write a brief letter of gratitude with whatever nice personal remarks you can think of addressed to all members of the family that will participate in looking after you.

2. Wake up at least one and one-half hours before your class starts. I do not know how much time it will take from home to the university, but plan accordingly and allow for this.

Be sure to clean the wash basin and bathtub each time after use. In the evening, always be cautious about making too much noise, such as by playing a radio or tape player, heavy footsteps and slamming doors or windows. Try not to create extra problems for the Bells or in the community.

3. On Mondays through Fridays, come home immediately after classes to study. Tell yourself: "Since I have good holidays during the weekends, today I will work hard."

During the weekends, allow some free time to spend with the Bells. When you go out to meet your friends, tell Professor Bell and Mrs. Bell beforehand where you will be and with whom.

Always plan to come home before the Bells' bedtime. In case you should miss that limit, telephone them before 8 or 9 p.m. Don't use the telephone for long chit-chats with friends. When necessary to contact us, call collect.

4. In classroom, always tell yourself: "I am curious." Do not think that learning is like filing documents in a cabinet. Be sure to use your brain for reasoning.

We all need wisdom along with knowledge. I believe the Bible is one of the most essential sources for this. Try to read at least one chapter of Proverbs and five from the Book of Psalms. This can be accomplished within a one month period.

Health and Safety:

1. Take good care of your health and avoid getting into unnecessary dangerous situations. Always calculate whether the risks you are taking are commensurate with the rewards. Think about ways that risks can be minimized; for instance, by sitting in the back of a car if there is no safety belt next to the driver's seat.

Be proud as you abide by traffic rules and school regulations. Some people boast about breaking orders of society. Do not be one of them.
2. Avoid carrying large sums of money on your person or flashing money about. Also avoid going into public parks at night, or parts of large cities which are seedy or ill-lit.
——Your father

Makoto is now a father with a beautiful family of his own living in Boston. Itaru would be very proud.

Having the Time of Your Life

When I believed that my existence was such a further fact, I seemed imprisoned in myself. My life seemed like a glass tunnel, through which I was moving faster every year, and at the end of which there was darkness. When I changed my view, the walls of my glass tunnel disappeared. I now live in the open air. There is still a difference between my life and the lives of other people. But the difference is less. Other people are closer. I am less concerned about the rest of my own life, and more concerned about the lives of others.
——Oxford Philosopher Derek Parfit[14]

From the time of our earliest ancestors, Man has looked to the heavens for guidance and inspiration. The Sun—source of life— governed seasons for hunting and signaled time to prepare shelter, clothing and food for winter's sovereignty. The Moon was a calendar for planting and harvesting as settlers asserted dominion over the wilderness. The stars were maps and compasses that led explorers on voyages which extended territorial domains.

---

[14] Derek Parfit, *Reasons and Persons,* 1984, Oxford Paperbacks

In these ways, and many more, the sky expressed the majesty and will of great powers that controlled human enterprise and destiny. It presented mysteries that raised human consciousness and stimulated self-reflection. It was the home of the human soul where mortal human achievements would ultimately find reward.

Advanced telescopes and space travel have brought some aspects of the heavens into closer view, yet mysteries of the human soul remain as elusive as ever. We now realize that the Moon, planets, Sun and stars are far more distant than our forefathers and foremothers perceived with unaided eyes. If this is where souls reside, then the space available for them to occupy is enormous.

But before we get too excited about the prospect of roaming around heaven all day, it might be interesting to consider different possibilities regarding a soul's essential nature. It seems that many people attach importance to the idea of having a soul, believing that life without one leads literally to a dead end.

Sharing Nature's Soul

Is the principal reason to live a good life to enable our souls to enjoy peace and contentment in an endless hereafter? If we believe the wrong things or behave badly, will our souls suffer eternal punishment?

I have serious difficulty with such concepts because I favor the idea that a mortal life is a blessing, not a test for something later, and that important joys and sorrows we experience are influenced in the here-and-now by the ways we respond to that reality. I can't comprehend any way to reward a soul, or to punish one either, for that matter. If souls are part of the Universe, they already have everything they could possibly need for satisfaction. And since I doubt that they have any corporeal nerve endings, eternal fires probably wouldn't hurt much.

Maybe their biggest problem would be boredom, but then again, there wouldn't be any clocks to watch in a cosmic time-space frame.

As a child, I imagined my soul to be like an invisible helium balloon in my head. The balloon contained my personality and my experiences, including memories of wonderful times and friendships. When I died, I expected that my balloon would be released to float up into the clouds—maybe even higher. It might be carried aloft by winds so that I could look down upon everything below.

I expected that there would be other balloons up there too, including all the people I loved and missed who had died. Since the balloons were transparent or ethereal, I would be able to see images of their former bodies inside, appearing as they looked when I knew them so that they could be recognized. Unfortunately, without physical bodies, we wouldn't be able to hug each other. That would be a sad and lonely feeling.

Later, another possibility occurred to me. Maybe there is only one soul, the soul of God, Nature, the Universe—whatever we choose to call it. As a metaphor, that soul would be like a big ocean containing all life. Like jellyfish, all creatures would be formed out of the water, as well as contain the precious liquid within. If those creatures were rational and self-reflective, they might believe they owned that seawater soul inside them. In reality, they would only be borrowing nutrients from that cosmic fluid which would eventually be released for others to use.

That early notion influenced me to realize that there is truly something more important to me than mortal survival. It is the promise that I am a spiritual extension of all life, and will continue to be so long as nature exists.

Does History Repeat Ourselves?

Even if there is that one universal soul, is there some aspect of me-ness and you-ness that gets recycled when that biodegradable part of our persona no longer serves its purpose? What about being reborn into a new and fresh body where we restart our mortal cycle? This general reincarnation concept has existed in various forms and religions for at least 3,000 years.

Ancient Greek philosophers wrote extensively about the concept of reincarnation, in connection with the legendary Orpheus and Pythagoras. Socrates apparently embraced the concept, writing:

> *If all things which partook of life were to die, and after they were dead remained in the form of death, and did not come to life again, all would at last die, and nothing be alive—what other result could there be? ... Must not all things at last be swallowed up in death? ... But I am confident that there truly is such a thing as living again, and that the living spring from the dead, and that the souls of the dead are in existence, and that good souls have a better portion than the evil.*[15]

Plato taught that one's soul is immortal, preexists before birth, and is reborn many times. He argued that each soul chooses its next life, guided by its experiences in the previous lives. His student Aristotle initially accepted this idea, but later largely rejected the concepts of reincarnation and immortality.

Although belief in reincarnation is not held as a mainstream concept in Judaism and Christianity, it has been recognized within some of their followers.

---

[15] *Encyclopedia of Death and Dying,* http://www.deathreference.com/Py-Se/Reincarnation.html

The *Kabbalah* body of teaching based upon an interpretation of Hebrew Scriptures includes this concept, and Hasidic Jews include it in their belief system as well.

Some early Christians, particularly the Gnostic Christians, believed in reincarnation, as did some groups in southern Europe, at least until the Council of Constantinople in 553 A.D. Even today some Christians find support for reincarnation in the passage in the *New Testament Book of Matthew* in which Jesus seems to say that John the Baptist is the prophet Elijah returned.

In Hinduism, it is believed that an enduring soul spends a variable amount of time in another realm following death before becoming associated with a new human or animal body of either sex. Karma determines the conditions into which one is reborn based upon conduct during previous lives. Since life on Earth is considered less than fully desirable, an individual can engage in religious practices in each life until eventually earning release from the rebirth cycle. This results upon achieving union with the infinite spirit, nirvana, whereupon personal individuality loses meaning.

In Theravada Buddhism found in southern parts of Asia, there is no enduring entity that persists from one life to the next. As emphasized in the doctrine of "anatta", or no soul, at the death of one personality a new one comes into being much like the flame of a dying candle can serve to light the flame of another. The new personality first emerges into a non-terrestrial plane of existence prior to becoming a terrestrial being.

Similar to Hinduism, the natural law of karma which is akin to laws of physics, determines circumstances of subsequent lives. Accordingly, there is continuity between personalities, but not persistence of identity. For this reason, Theravada Buddhists prefer the term "rebirth" to "reincarnation". Such circumstances of rebirths are not perceived as rewards or punishments handed out by a controlling God, but rather are natural results of various good deeds and misdeeds. The rebirth cycle involve innumerable lives including both sexes and nonhuman animals over many eons. This continues until all cravings are lost and nirvana is achieved.

Unlike Hindus and Buddhists, many religious populations in West Africa believe that individual rebirth is desirable and that life on Earth is preferable to that of the discarnate, limbo state. Some believe that individuals are generally reborn into the same family, and that souls may even split into several rebirths simultaneously. Included are "repeater children," in which one soul will harass a family by repeatedly dying as an infant or young child only to be reborn into the family again. Some groups also accept the possibility of rebirth into nonhuman animals, while others do not.

Many Inuit tribes, particularly those in northern and northwestern parts of North America, hold reincarnation concepts which vary greatly across different groups. As with certain West African groups, some believe that an individual can be reborn simultaneously as different people within the same family. Birthmarks corresponding to wounds of dead warriors are given as special credence.

Depending upon the tribe, it isn't necessarily expected that all deceased individuals will be reborn, or that rebirth will necessarily assume same-sex or human form.

Various Shiite Muslim groups in western Asia such as the Druses of Lebanon and Syria and the Alevis in Turkey believe in personal reincarnation without the Hindu or Buddhist concept of karma. Instead, God assigns souls to a series of lives in different circumstances that remain disconnected from one another until the ultimate Judgment Day when they are consigned to heaven or hell based upon the moral quality of their lifetime actions.

While the Alevis believe that rebirth can occur in nonhuman animal forms, the Druses do not, and in fact believe they can only be reborn as Druses. Neither group believes that rebirth can be to an opposite sex.

Larry Bell

My Childhood Soul Balloons

As a child I tried to contemplate what my soul would do
after it emerged somewhere from my body when I died.
I first imagined that it would float up into the clouds in
a balloon, perhaps even higher, where I would be
reunited with other souls of other departed people and
creatures that had been important parts of my life.
I later began to wonder whether my soul and theirs
might eventually tend to get a little bored. After all,
eternity seemed like a very long time to spend simply
reminiscing about past relationships and experiences.

Soulprints from the Past?

In 1961 Canadian-born American psychologist Ian Stevenson, then the chairman of the Department of Psychiatry at the University of Virginia, began investigating cases of young children from all over the world, Asia in particular, who claimed to remember previous lives. Since that time, he and other researchers have collected over 2,500 cases of such children.[16]

Examples were most prevalently found in cultures with a belief in reincarnation, including India, Sri Lanka, Turkey, Lebanon, Thailand, Myanmar, West Africa, and among the tribal groups of northwest North America. However cases have been found wherever they have been sought, including more than 100 nontribal American instances.

While individual experiences evidenced significant variations, they also generally appeared to share certain characteristics. In a typical case, a child at the age of two or three might begin to speak spontaneously about another life, sometimes describing the life of a stranger, while others talked about a deceased individual known to the child's family.

In such cases involving a stranger, the child might persist with claims until their family eventually made efforts to locate the family of the previous personality whose life the child was describing. When these efforts were successful the child would then meet the family and often be said to identify members of the previous family along with items belonging to the deceased individual.

Most often, the children reporting past lives described someone in their own culture or at least with some geographical

---

[16] Dr. *Ian Stevenson's Reincarnation Research,* Kevin Williams, Near Death Experiences,
http://www.near death.com/experiences/reincarnation01.html

connection. Burmese children, for example might describe lives of Japanese soldiers killed there during World War II. Cases of children describing lives in faraway countries were very rare. Those lives were most typically ordinary ones involving routine occupations, with links to a famous person or royalty essentially non-existent.

Stevenson found that approximately 60 percent of the deaths commonly referred to were violent in nature. Nearly three-quarters of the subjects described the mode of death of the previous personality. Much of the memory emphasis was upon events that took place near the end of the previous life. A child describing the life of an adult tended to talk about a spouse or children rather than referring to parents.

And whereas the average interval between the death of a previous personality and the birth of the child is about fifteen months, those of a violent nature had a shorter interval. Many showed extreme emotion and wept when they talked about missing their previous family. Some showed great anger in describing their killer one minute, and then went off to play the next.

About half of the children reporting a violent end showed phobias related to the mode of death. Sometimes that phobia was present long before the child talked about the previous life; for example, a child reporting a memory of drowning in a previous life may have exhibited an intense fear of water as a baby.

Perhaps most bizarre, about 35 percent of the child subjects reportedly bore a birthmark or birth defect that matched a wound of the previous personality, usually the fatal wound. Moreover, the birthmarks often tended to be unusual, including puckered scar-like areas. In the late 1990s Stevenson published a series of over 200 such cases in which the marks corresponded to wound types and locations based upon postmortem reports and other records.

While some children described experiences of past lives of staying near their home or the site of their deaths, even witnessing the funerals, others reported going to a discarnate realm. Some described meetings with other beings such as sages or guides.

Most of the subjects began talking about previous lives between ages two and five years, and stopped talking about previous lives by age eight. That's when they branched out from family to begin school, and when the children tended to lose early childhood memories.

Do these observations offer conclusive evidence that childhood memories can or do reveal previous lives? Taken at face value, do they prove that that, emotions, a sense of identification, and even physical features can carry over from one life to the next? Let's briefly consider some other possibilities that offer plausible reasons for skepticism.

One explanation is fraud. Yet by all indications Dr. Stevenson and his team were experienced and reputable researchers who would not either perpetrate fraud, or fail to recognize its existence over the course of their expansive investigations.

Could many of those children have learned about the deceased person through normal means, but then later forgotten where they acquired the information? Perhaps, except that the investigations typically failed to turn up any evidence suggesting that children had any opportunities to hear or know anything about the previous personality. Nor does it explain the strong sense of identification with the previous personality and other behavioral features that the children often showed. In fact, results indicate that the stronger cases expressing more verified statements about the previous life tend to involve greater distance between the homes of the child and the previous personality than the weaker ones.

A third possibility is that information became exaggerated after the families of the subject and the previous personality have met. This might have subsequently occurred through faulty memory on the part of the participants. According to this interpretation, the evidence for a connection with a previous life is not valid due to faulty memory over time on the part of the participants.

This scenario might be accorded more weight were it not for studies conducted by Stevenson and parapsychologist Jürgen Keil which reinvestigated initial cases twenty years later. They found that the cases had not become stronger in the participants' minds over the years, and, in fact, some had become somewhat weaker as witnesses recalled less specific details of what the child had said.

Finally, is it possible that children, and perhaps all of us, can gain knowledge of others, living and dead through something termed "extrasensory perception?"

Larry Bell

Do Souls get Recycled?

The general concept of reincarnation, while common to many religions and cultures, has a variety of interpretations. Hasidic Jews and even Gnostic Christians subscribed to a belief that humans recurrently return in human form. In Hinduism the enduring soul may be reborn either as a person or animal based on karma, their conduct during their previous lives.

Theravada Buddhists prefer the term "rebirth" to reincarnation where there is no persistence of personalities. Cycles continue repeatedly, including human and animal forms.

Paranormal Propositions

I'm willing to bet that most of us experience what seem to be extrasensory events in our lives which are impossible to rationally understand. One that comes to my mind involved a "connection" with someone I had served with in the military nearly two decades earlier. Although Ken and I were never really close pals, we got along together just fine. Still, I couldn't imagine any good reason to be thinking about him when he "popped into my head". I was traveling and busy at the time, and the thought prompted me to make a mental note to give him a call when I returned home. One week later I did so.

Although I didn't have a telephone number, I did recall that his family had an electrical appliance store in Milwaukee, and correctly took a chance that it might be listed in his surname. Asking to speak to Ken, the person who answered introduced himself as his brother. He informed me that Ken had died a week earlier.

On another occasion I decided to call an out-of-town friend that I hadn't seen for many years, and again for no particular reason. When I did so, the line was busy. He was calling me.

So how could such unlikely coincidences have occurred? Well perhaps for the same reason that infinitely more coincidences didn't, or at least that we didn't happen to notice them.

Being of generally skeptical nature, I can offer some reasons that the second answer might most often be warranted. At the same time, to group such experiences into terms like "paranormal" or "supernatural" naively suggests that we have a handle on what normal or natural really is, or in other words, that existing physical science, psychology or philosophy already explains everything. On the other hand, spiritualism - a belief that one can be in contact with a spiritual realm - is also problematic given that hard evidence is difficult when we don't understand what we are investigating.

As Michael Shermer, an American science writer and noted skeptic of supernatural claims stated in 2002, the definition of science is:

A set of methods designed to describe and interpret observed or inferred phenomena, past or present, and aimed at building a testable body of knowledge open to rejection or confirmation. [17]

Presumably, the more unconventional or controversial the inferred phenomena, the more rigorous must be those tests. Scottish philosopher David Hume summarized this stating *"Extraordinary claims require extraordinary evidence."* On the other hand, Carl Sagan in *The Demon-Haunted World* also reminds us that *"absence of evidence is not evidence of absence."*

It is quite apparent that there are people who capitalize upon public gullibility to sell paranormal-premised theories, such as using scientific-sounding terms such as "energy fields" or "frequencies" to explain spirit world contacts and occurrences which many wish to believe. In fact so many people took up ghost hunting following the popular 1984 movie *Ghostbusters* that Edmund Scientific began marketing an "EMF Ghost Meter" (low-frequency microwave or radio wave electromagnetic field detector) to determine if certain premises are "haunted."

By all measures, business must be good. As Arthur C. Clark facetiously observes in 2001: A Space Odyssey:

Beyond every man now stands 30 ghosts, for that is the ratio by which dead outnumber the living.

Clark also told us:

---

[17] Scientific American, *Smart People Believe in Weird Things*, September, 2002

Two possibilities exist: Either we are alone in the Universe or we are not. Both are equally terrifying.

It seems perfectly natural to seek answers to questions of a spiritual and metaphysical realm that offer encouragement and comfort. When a loved one dies, we long for hope that we might see them again. Nor is it easy for most of us to contemplate our own final mortality...a world without us in it.

As Darwin wrote:

> *The belief in unseen or spiritual agencies...seems to be almost universal...nor is it difficult to comprehend how it arose. As soon as the important faculties of imagination, wonder, and curiosity, together with the power of reasoning, had become partially developed, man would naturally have craved to understand what was passing around him, and have vaguely speculated on his own existence.*[18]

In his 1818 work *The World as Will and Representation*, German philosopher Arthur Schopenhauer attributes this curiosity and wonderment to a natural stage of intellectual development:

> *The lower a man is in an intellectual respect, the less puzzling and mysterious existence itself is to him; on the contrary, everything, how it is and that it is, seems to him a matter of course.*

The Elusive Quest for Rationality

"Rationality" can be defined as the quality or state of being "reasonable" with regard to conformity between one's beliefs and actions depending upon available information and facts. Some seek

---

[18] *The Descent of Man, and Selection in Relation to Sex*, Charles Darwin, (1886)

it in the infallible and immutable teachings of religious dogma and scripture. Some turn to hypotheses and insights of philosophers. Some place primary hope and trust in provable scientific theorems. And some, perhaps most of us spread their bets, counting on informative revelations from all three.

The German sociologist Max Weber distinguished between four types of rationality. The first, which he called "Zweckrational" is related to the expectations about the behavior of other human beings or objects in the environment which serve as means for a particular actor to attain ends which Weber noted were "rationally pursued and calculated."

Weber called the second type "Wertrational" or value/belief-oriented whereby action is undertaken for what one might call reasons intrinsic to the actor. These include ethical, aesthetic, religious or other motive, independent of whether it will lead to success. Added to these are "affectual" rationality determined by an actor's specific affect, feeling, or emotion—to which Weber characterized as being on the borderline of being "meaningfully oriented"; and a fourth type determined largely by ingrained habituation. Webster emphasized that combinations were the norm, and considered the first two more significant than the others.

An advantage of Weber's interpretation of rationality is that it avoids a value-laden assessment that certain kinds of beliefs are irrational. Instead, Weber suggests that a ground or motive can be given—for religious or affect reasons, for example.

Some philosophers believe however that a "good" rationale must be independent of personal emotions, feelings of instincts. Accordingly, any process of evaluation or analysis is expected to be logical and free of subjective bias.

Immanuel Kant distinguished theoretical from practical reason depending upon whether they apply the thoughts they accept to the actions they perform. Here, theoretical rationality can be said to regulate our beliefs, while practical rationality is the strategy for living one's best possible life to achieve most important goals and preferences.

So after all, allowing for different definitions and interpretations, what is truly rationale in contemplating two basic aspects of metaphysical existence—namely what is ultimately "there" (or "here")?; and what is it really like? Or stated another way, which perceptions are "irrational"?

Readily accepting license afforded me by Webster to apply personal philosophical and experience-based values, I regard the concept of a vengeful God who punishes souls of disbelievers and moral transgressors in an afterlife to be both irrational and highly disagreeable.

As an adolescent youth attending protestant religious services I was deeply disturbed to witness a dramatic film presentation targeted upon young audiences which graphically depicted sinners being tormented in hell. My reaction was that use of such a device to terrify impressionable young minds into accepting such doctrine was fundamentally immoral on its face. I never returned to that church.

I also reject any notion that fear of punishment trumps a desire to lead ethical lives in civilized societies. The conventional wisdom that what goes around comes around applies to doing good onto others as we would have them do onto us, not just unfortunate consequences of bad actions. To believe otherwise denies rational virtues of human empathy, compassion and generosity.

Is it less rational to believe in Spinoza's God who reveals himself in orderly harmony rather than one who concerns himself with critically judging the affairs and actions of human beings? If so, why did He devote so much attention to creating an endless variety of dinosaurs and other now-extinct creatures long before humans arrived on the scene? Was that meteorological cue ball on the species adaptation gene pool table part of a divine plan all along, or just a random cosmological event? In any case, it was a fortuitous game-changer for mammals such as us.

Subscription to contemporary scientific theories often requires that we suspend conventional perceptions of what seems rational also. Like trying to imagine that the entire Universe of suns, planets and gerbils began as a singularity smaller than an atom which banged its way out of virtual nonexistence. Or conceiving of a time before time existed and gravity gave it a closed shape. Makes religion seem pretty tame doesn't it?

And what about quantum mechanics...the notion that conventional laws of physics break down when elements of the system being studied get really, really tiny? If this is "mysterious", does the mystery lie in why there are two different and contradictory sets of laws, or more fundamentally why our traditional world-view sense of realty doesn't comport with what is being observed?

What if as some scientists theorize, instead of a one-world perception whereby tiny blobs of particle presence appear to race around linearly in physical space with a particular position and momentum, there are simultaneously two-worlds which allow those blobs to simultaneously take multiple paths.

As Einstein argued based upon single-global-world interpretations of quantum physics of his era, experiments which produce single unique results violate special relativity. They impose a preferred space of simultaneity and require a mysterious influence to be transferred faster than light, which mysterious influence can't be used to transmit useful information. Getting rid of the single-global-world assumption normalizes this mystery.[19]

That multi-world concept is a theoretical mathematical construct, an abstraction that enables visualization of an allegorical Platonic world revealed through shadows of reality projected on our cave wall of understanding. As Jim Holt explains:

---

[19] *Quantum Physics Revealed as Non-Mysterious*, Elizer Yudkowsky, June 12, 2008, Lesswrong Blog

...when physicists and philosophers talk about two different regions of spacetime being 'two Universes,' what they generally mean is that those regions are 1) very, very large; 2) causally isolated from each other; 3) mutually unknowable by direct observation. [20]

Those separate Universes can hypothetically have a variety of optional spatial dimensions, operate simultaneously in different regions of spacetime as "parallel Universes", and even manifest different alter egos of ourselves.

Is this "logical"? If experimental evidence based upon theories of quantum mechanics suggest that it "works", does this make it at least plausible?

A popular axiom in analytical discourse applies the "KISS" principle...Keep it Simple, Stupid. A respected scientific corollary of this, "Occam's razor", is a problem-solving principle which states that among competing hypotheses, the one with the fewest assumptions should be selected. Other, more complicated solutions may ultimately prove correct, but—in the absence of certainty—the fewer assumptions that are made, the better.

Keeping things simple—avoiding tiresome and confusing complexity—is seductive because it makes our busy lives more manageable. If people we respect or carry the mantel of authority tell us that something is logical, it is tempting to believe them...particularly if their explanations satisfy beliefs and actions which are appealing.

We also tend to trust our senses to inform us about what is "real". This tends to work for us most of the time also. Yet while we tend to think that stones are hard, snow is cold and grass is green, laws of physics inform us otherwise. Everything we perceive as hard is made of tiny bits of energetic stuff that has no "solidity" at all; the temperature we sense is but specific electromagnetic

---

[20] *Why Does the World Exist*, Ibid

frequencies and wavelengths detected by neurons and calibrated by our brains to inform us about our surroundings; and color perception is an interpretative phenomena as well. Yellow light, for example, describes transversal electromagnetic wavelengths in the neighborhood of 590 nanometers.

Those images we "see" in front of us are really illusory constructs which are assembled behind our eyes in our brains. The sensory impressions of taste and smell depend upon specialized chemical receptors that differentiate between presence of different molecules or ions. Hearing, a mechanical process, relates to how our brains interpret various vibrations within the range of our audio detectors caused when something moves air around.

We don't have to understand how these things work, or why, for that matter as Einstein deduced from his special relativity theory that $E=mc^2$... that the mass of an object or system which is reliant upon the speed of light is a measure of its energy content. The important thing from a practical perspective is that they seem simple, particularly if you're a rocket scientist, and they do work. Or at least they do until quantum mechanics messes things up and makes them more complicated again.

On the subject of messing up simple theories, what about the possibility that an individual's "mind-soul" becomes demented by age and infirmity prior to death? Is that impaired or incoherent personality often experienced in late years the enduring one that survives or reincarnates? Does some "divine selector" pick and choose the "true you" out of all the personal change phases of life?

Sorry, but I just couldn't help but wonder.

The Changing Nature of Reason

Thou shalt not suffer a witch to live.
Exodus 22:18, from King James Bible Version

You shall not permit a sorceress to live.

Exodus 22:18, English Standard Bible Version

A man or woman who is a medium or spiritist among you must be put to death. You are to stone them; their blood will be on their own heads.
Leviticus 20:27, New International Bible Version

Had we lived in Europe six centuries ago, or more recently in Salem, Massachusetts two centuries later, some really bad things befell many who were accused of cavorting with the devil in spiritualist practices claimed to have afflicted people and cattle with diseases, caused crop failures, or were attributed to other calamities. Barbaric penalties such as death by stoning or being burned at the stake were not only permitted, but were strongly sanctioned by the general populace as moral responsibilities.

As Voltaire noted:

Those who can make you believe absurdities can make you commit atrocities.

Claremont Graduate University and Chapman University Adjunct Professor Michael Shermer makes a case that such actions could be deemed rational during those earlier times based upon mistaken beliefs about how laws of nature and morality work. In his new book *The Moral Arc: How Science and Reason Lead Humanity toward Truth, Justice and Freedom*, he supports this logic with a thought experiment. Here, Shermer asks each of us to consider how we would respond to the following scenario:

Imagine that you are standing next to a fork in a railroad line with a switch. A runaway trolley car is about to kill five workers on the track — unless you throw the switch to divert the trolley down the side track where it will kill only one worker. He then asks, "Would you kill one to save five?" [21]

Predicting that most of us would throw that switch, Shermer argues that medieval witch-burners performed the same kind of moral calculation under a false utilitarian assumption that it was better to kill a few to save many. He points out that the primary difference between then and now is, in a word, "science".

Operating in an information vacuum, the witch executors had no systematic method, therefore no clue, to determine a correct course of action. Fortunately, that witch theory of causality was subsequently debunked through scientific inquiry. Over the centuries new science has also led to much broader improvements of humanity along with (or consequence of) gradual replacement of religious supernaturalism with scientific naturalism.

Shermer attributes this moral progress along with a "general application of scientific reason in all fields" to two intellectual revolutions. The first was a Scientific Revolution dating roughly from the 1543 publication of Copernicus's *On the Revolution of Heavenly Spheres,* to the 1687 publication of Isaac Newton's *Principia Mathematica.* This revolution led directly to the second, the "Age of Reason and Enlightenment" dating from that time to the French Revolution in 1795.

Both revolutions laid foundations for 18th century thinkers to apply rigorous natural science and philosophical disciplines in attempts to explain phenomena previously left to be addressed within theological domains, Scottish philosopher David Hume referred to this marriage of science and philosophy as a "science of man."

As Michel Shermer observes, it was Newton's *Principia* that provided the "watershed event that changed everything", an achievement declared by his contemporary, the great French

---

[21] *The Moral Arc: How Science and Reason lead humanity toward Truth, Justice and Freedom,* New York: Henry Holt, 2015.

mathematician and astronomer Joseph-Louis Lagrange, to be "the premier production of the human mind." The prominent 19th century French mathematical physicist and astronomer Pierre-Simon Laplace referred to Newton's accomplishments as "a pre-eminence above all other productions of the human intellect."

Newton's deductive method also influenced French philosopher Baron de La Brèdeet de Montesquieu. In his 1748 work *Del'espirit de lois* (The Spirit of the Law), Montesquieu speculated that exposure of different societies to customs and manners different from their own leads to "a cure for the most destructive prejudices." He and others among a group of French scientists and scholars known as "physiocrats" believed that all social facts are linked together by "immutable, ineluctable, and inevitable laws". They argued that all human societies are regulated by the same natural laws that govern the physical world, animal societies, and even the internal life of every organism.

Motivated by abundant natural curiosity and guided by disciplined scientific and philosophical queries, followers of Newton's example dating back to the Scientific Revolution and Age of Reason and Enlightenment have dared to challenge bonds and inertia of powerful orthodox authorities. In doing so, they continue to open our awareness to new worlds of understanding and possibility. Or as Michael Shermer puts it, their ongoing discoveries inform us how to "do more to elevate humanity, extend the moral arc, and bend it ever upward."

Unleashing Natural Curiosity

Dangers of curiosity regarding life's eternal questions were well recognized by Mankind long before it allegedly killed a cat somewhere. This has been clear from the time that a snake-in-the-grass tempted Adam and Eve with classified information divinely reserved for members of the theological elite. History is replete with other examples as well, including Benjamin Franklin's dumb thunderstorm kite flying experiment, and a peeping Tom in Poughkeepsie who reportedly was nearly bludgeoned to death by an irate husband.

In fairness, however, there have also been episodes when too little curiosity has caused serious problems. One that immediately comes to mind was an occasion when Trojan soldiers should have looked a large Greek gift horse in the mouth.

One of the most troublesome aspects of curiosity is that you can never be certain where it will lead. When allowed to get out of hand it can cause people to challenge conventional wisdom, and in extreme cases, even question the wisdom of many conventions. It can seduce us to question things that authorities tell us have already been established as truths, diverting attention away from dictates they agree on.

While really curious people face the risk of not fitting in, some exceptions are made for scientists because they occasionally stumble onto discoveries that are useful. Besides, since they spend most of their time in laboratories or attending conferences there isn't much opportunity for them to get into trouble. Artists often have curiosity too, and seem to question just about everything most of the rest of us take for granted. Sometimes they come up with ideas and observations that are interesting; even beautiful. The rest of the time they usually stick to their own misunderstood and underappreciated business.

Let's face it, people with overactive curiosity often tend to be somewhat eccentric. Others who pretty much know what they believe about everything are much more solid and reliable. We might think of them as concentric because we can generally understand where they are coming from, where they are going, and where they are most likely to wind up.

On the other hand, nearly all of us have both of these characteristics to some degree. We all believe certain things. By this I'm referring to things that we really care about. So I'm not addressing those sorts of circumstances when we might say, for example, "I believe I'll have another helping of that delicious pecan pie." No one particularly cares about that unless it is the last piece. Instead, I'm referring to the kind of belief that represents true faith.

For instance, we believe in certain principles we have learned to value and trust. We believe in lessons and ideas that inspire and guide us in seeking higher, more productive possibilities in our lives. We believe in dreams and goals that give us hope and motivate us to pursue worthwhile relationships and enterprises. Such beliefs offer foundations and references to better understand ourselves and others, as well as providing compasses to direct us towards well-lived lives.

Are curiosity and belief polar opposites? Is curiosity, by nature, open, and belief, by necessity closed? I don't *believe* so. Instead, I think that both are interdependent. Curiosity reveals experiences and options that enable us to make more informed choices regarding what we believe. Belief, on the other hand, gives curiosity substance to work on. Belief, in fact, can motivate curiosity to explore broader dimensions of meaning. In this sense, belief should truly be an open system too.

Perhaps the greatest risk of curiosity occurs when we neglect it and allow ourselves to blindly and steadfastly cling to unsupported precepts and preconceptions. Without curiosity we are also likely to miss out on unexpected adventures of thought and experience which enrich life and make it more exciting. So why not go ahead, accept curiosity's lesser dangers, and just try to enjoy our mortal adventure – wherever it leads?

So Where Does All of This Finally Leave Us?

Again, back to the beginning…what happens when the stage lights dim and the curtains close on our life dramas?

The quintessential public stage showman and conjurer Harry Houdini became interested in this question following his beloved mother's death in 1913. However, after attending several psychic medium sessions in attempts to communicate with her he concluded that all were frauds. Houdini and his wife then worked to expose secret tricks used to exploit grieving people by conducting séances of their own, along with debunking explanations in two books: *Miracle Mongers and Their Methods*, (1920) and *A Magician Among the Spirits* (1924).

Before Houdini himself died, he and his wife Bess agreed that if possible he would communicate the message "Rosabelle believe", the title of their favorite song, using a secret code. Here, the results present some continuing adversarial controversy between spirit-communication believers and skeptics.

Bess held annual séances for ten years following Houdini's death. After claiming in 1929 that spiritualist Arthur Ford had successfully contacted her husband, she later stated that the incident had been faked. In 1936 following a tenth and final séance on the roof of the Knickerbocker Hotel she blew out a candle that had been burning next to Houdini's photograph since the time of his death. Bess said that "ten years is long enough to wait for any man."

Just as Houdini's denial of spiritualism came at the cost of his former close friendship with Sir Arthur Conan Doyle, a firm believer, skepticism of other life-after-death phenomena such as vivid, detailed out-of-body experiences will offend others who hold these visions. Which views can we trust to be fully objective and rational? I'll leave this for others to speculate.

But if the answer to a scientist asking why quantum phenomena doesn't follow special relativity—or a child asking "who created God?"—is that "God works in mysterious ways", who can presently argue with that? Jim Holt takes such mysteries even further, essentially asking "why does anything exist?" Here the answer would require not only understanding what God is and what God wants, but also how each of us fits into that picture.

As Holt quotes John Updike observing: "Conceptually, the question 'why does the world exist?' rhymes with 'why do I exist?'"

Russian writer Ivan Goncharov may have provided the only answer we need in his 1859 novel *Oblomov*: "The purpose is to live."

Whatever God's script for each of us on the cosmic stage of life, there's every reason to believe that the show must go on. After all, if our present knowable lifetime is but a random sampling of eternity, is it likely to occur only now and at no other time? Yet if this current stage show offers an encore or sequel, what characters will each of us play...or who will play us?

And what part of us will have a role to play? Since our physical biological selves will already have been used up, what part of us will survive? Will our personalities and egos which we assembled over a few brief decades hang around throughout eternity? Won't memories become static, stale and expendable? What will really be worth keeping? What about hoping instead for a chance to really start over...new experiences...new potentials? Isn't that the benefit that the gift of life offers?

Think again about someone who has amnesia...where identity is ambiguous, memories are lost, but potentials for new experiences and growth remain. Isn't that a whole lot better than being dead?

Maybe it's a good news/bad news story after all. The good news is that life is an ongoing adventure...a voyage to endless times and places. The bad news is simply that we can't pack our old albums and scrapbooks.

On the other hand, maybe traveling light is actually a good thing too?

No, You Really Can't take it with You

Just as you didn't come into this life burdened with old
baggage, why should fresh start opportunities in the
next one be different? Perhaps recognize that change is
the true Nature of the living Universe and be grateful to
be included.

Epilogue

One day when I was with my sister and brother-in-law, our conversation somehow turned to the somber question of where we would want our mortal remains to be put. When I was queried on this, I replied that it really didn't matter at all. Just find any pretty place to scatter my ashes and that will be perfectly fine. Then it occurred to me that this subject was really part of a larger issue which revolved around where I considered my *real* home to be. If I were to choose one particular place that is most important in my life, where is it? I'm still thinking about that.

Many places have been very special to me. All evoke memories of wonderful people, happy and trying times, landscapes and buildings—a flood of clear and half-remembered images. Each of those places hold important experiences that are part of me. How could I choose between them?

Would I pick the small Midwestern town where I spent my childhood and high school years? That's where I first discovered joys and challenges of friendship, experimented with romance, acquired formative lessons and values, was first exposed to responsibility, and enjoyed fun and adventures which were not all known to my parents.

And what about all those other places? Places where I was stationed in the military, attended universities, fell in love and became married, experienced my own children, pursued interests and achievements, and encountered people and possibilities that have had strong and lasting influences. The place where I live now holds many of those memories, along with current realities.

Over the years, for one reason or another, I have visited locales where I have lived before, often perhaps with hopeful anticipation of rediscovering the home and life I once knew. Each time I was disappointed to realize that it no longer existed. Most of the people I had known were gone. Settings that I had enjoyed had changed beyond recognition. Even broader landscapes seemed somewhat unfamiliar or alien due to a wide range of subsequent developments.

My feelings of attachment and disillusionment have been strongest when I have returned to my home town of childhood. There are still powerful attractions that draw me there. The farmlands and natural countryside are beautiful. The private airport that my parents built and operated much of their lives still exists, now as an active municipal facility. A circular paved and landscaped memorial site that I created for them there originally contained two sentinel trees to symbolize my parents still together, standing side-by-side. The earth containing those trees, now harsh winter casualties, berms up to the top of a curved retaining wall which forms a bench overlooking a runway; a place where people can rest and watch airplanes. Mom's and dad's ashes are buried there, and I feel comforted and close to them when I visit that place.

But the area has changed in many ways that are difficult for me to adjust to. Just up the highway from the airport where I had spent many youthful years, a large gambling casino has been built on formerly rural land. The place is packed with people throughout the day and night, and has become a major employment center where local small town residents work among bow-tied blackjack dealers and net-stockinged waitresses.

The nearby state park where we roamed freely and partied boisterously at all hours is now crowded with tourists. It once had private cottages which are gone, and is now publicly controlled with tightly regimented rules that include closing hours. I doubt that many local residents go there anymore. Fast food franchises and large commercial outlets have drained business away from friendly mom-and-pop restaurants and stores I remember, and most of them have disappeared. So much for nostalgia!

Maybe it is a blessing that we really can't go back to recapture our past. After all, what's so bad about the present? As wonderful as those memories are, they don't offer the vitality or excitement of anticipation that we experience in our current lives.

The past is like a marvelous book we have already read. We have enjoyed and learned from it—and perhaps some new lessons are revealed when we read it again. One of those lessons is probably that we can't ever go back. Another is that *home* is really where we live among people who still need us and events we are still part of.

Let the ashes fall where they will.

Afterwords

A depressing spectacle unfolded on March 11, 2015 as I observed the leader of a surgical team at Methodist Hospital in Houston preparing the family of a newly admitted colon cancer patient for ominous circumstances. Preliminary diagnostic assessments of the father's prognosis were not encouraging. The large size of the malignancy suggested that it had advanced undetected over a period of several years, suggesting a strong likelihood that it had already spread beyond the original site.

Feeling more like a spectator rather than the featured attraction it was nearly unfathomable to grasp the realization that he was actually referring to me. I watched as the eldest of my two adult sons openly wept while the other, palm against forehead, registered grim disbelief. Nancy, my beloved partner in the best and worst of times appeared attentive to every word, expecting, as is her nature, that the next ones would support more optimism.

Blessedly, those welcome words came about two weeks later when immediately upon awakening from surgical anesthesia my coordinating physician told me "Larry, wonderful news! You are now free of cancer!" That truly caring soul made certain that I would receive this buoyant message without delay.

So far, she's pretty close to right. Subsequent analyses by expert oncologists at two top level independent hospitals, Methodist and the globally renowned M.D. Anderson Cancer, both project an 80 percent chance that there will be no future recurrence. Upon removal and examination there was no evidence to suggest that the malignancy had spread, and my somewhat shorter remaining innards were thankfully reconnected just fine.

Curiously, all of this unexpected development occurred but weeks after I had submitted the previous parts of this manuscript to my publisher. What prompted me to formally explore and chronicle related thoughts about mortality which date back over most of my lifetime? What have I learned from the experience of intellectually and emotionally confronting my mortality up close and personal? Did some consequential reality check warrant abandonment or editing of my previous book content?

No, other than adding these experiences, I haven't found reason to change anything.

But yes, there are at least a couple of personal lessons that are perhaps worth sharing after all. One is a reminder to displace conscious thoughts about mortality altogether by concentrating full attention to living. Another is that whatever certainty I may ultimately gain about life after self I'm presently in no big hurry to know. Like you, I have an eternity to explore those revelations.

Index

About the Author

LARRY BELL IS an endowed professor at the University of Houston where he founded the Sasakawa International Center for Space Architecture (SICSA) and the graduate program in space architecture. He is the author of *Climate of Corruption: Politics and Power Behind the Global Warming Hoax*, *Cosmic Musings: Contemplating Life Beyond Self* and more than 400 online articles on a wide variety of topics as a *Forbes* and *Newsmax* Contributor, some of which have also been featured in their hard-copy magazine publications.

Larry's professional aerospace work and interviews have appeared in numerous TV and print media productions which include the *History Channel*, *Discovery Channel-Canada*, *NASA Select* and leading national and international newspapers, popular magazines and professional journals. His many awards include certificates of appreciation from NASA Headquarters and two highest honors for his contributions to international space development awarded by Russia's leading aerospace society.

CPSIA information can be obtained
at www.ICGtesting.com
Printed in the USA
FFHW020007170119
50175623-55104FF